ANALYZING
ENVIRONMENTAL
CHANGE

ANALYZING THE
FOOD SUPPLY
CHAIN

ASKING QUESTIONS, EVALUATING EVIDENCE, AND DESIGNING SOLUTIONS

PHILIP STEELE

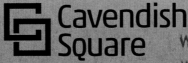

Cavendish
Square

New York

Published in 2019 by Cavendish Square
Publishing, LLC, 243 5th Avenue, Suite 136,
New York, NY 10016

Copyright © 2017 Wayland, a division of
Hachette Children's Group

First Edition

Cataloging-in-Publication Data

Names: Steele, Philip.
Title: Analyzing the food supply chain:
asking questions, evaluating evidence, and
designing solutions / Philip Steele.
Description: New York : Cavendish Square,
2019. | Series: Analyzing environmental
change | Includes glossary and index.
Identifiers: ISBN 9781502639479 (library
bound) | ISBN 9781502639486 (pbk.) | ISBN
9781502639493 (ebook)
Subjects: LCSH: Food supply--Social
aspects--Juvenile literature. | Consumption
(Economics)--Moral and ethical aspects--
Juvenile literature. | Food industry and
trade--Social aspects--Juvenile literature.
Classification: LCC HD9000.5 S834 2019 |
DDC 338.1'9--dc23

Produced for Cavendish Square by
Tall Tree Ltd
Editors: Jon Richards
Designers: Ed Simkins

Printed in the United States of America

CONTENTS

IT'S TIME TO TALK ABOUT FOOD

We wake up in the morning and smell… breakfast! Our senses send messages to the brain throughout the day: "I'm hungry," "That looks tasty," "I feel thirsty." Our bodies have evolved over millions of years into perfect food processors. Which is good news, because food and water keep us alive and healthy.

Many regions can produce a wide range of food products, as seen at this market in Malaysia, without having to import produce.

INDUSTRIAL FARMING
Today, many wealthy countries grow their food on large farms where crops are harvested and animals are raised on an industrial scale.

THE NEED TO FEED
The struggle to find or grow food is as old as human history. It started with the first hunters and gatherers. It continued with the first people to cook over a fire, and the first farmers to grow wheat or rice. Today we can eat so many kinds of food and process them in so many ways that our ancestors would have been amazed.

OVERCROWDED
Some intensive farming methods are thought of by many people as cruel, such as the raising of battery hens.

DISCONNECTED

People can now taste regional dishes from around the world at their local restaurants. There has never been more interest in television cooking shows and in celebrity chefs. But at home, fewer people sit around the table for a family meal. The average person is very detached from the land that produces the food, and from farming. A 2016 survey by a UK supermarket found that about 40 percent of young children didn't know that their breakfast egg came from a hen.

TOO LITTLE
About 11 percent of people throughout the world are undernourished.

TOO MUCH
Many people in developed countries are eating too much, especially foods that are high in sugar. As a result levels of obesity are soaring in these nations.

As the world's population grows, opinions differ as to how we can produce enough to feed everyone. In each chapter of this book we'll look at different aspects of the topic of food, exploring and discussing the issues involved. There are many vital questions to discuss.

Let's talk about them.

DEBATES ON A PLATE

The media often reports on food problems. One week the headlines say that one type of food is bad for us. The next week they tell us the opposite. Some people shrug their shoulders, but others look into it more closely. What we eat, and whether it is good for us, really is an important question.

JUST FOR STARTERS

There are all sorts of other debates going on as well. There are ethical questions about animal welfare, and whether we should eat meat or become vegetarians. That debate moves on to questions about how we use the land, because raising cattle is generally less efficient than growing crops. And that leads on to one of the most urgent questions of all. With the world's population growing so fast, how will we grow enough food for all these people? Throughout history, a shortage of basic or staple foods has triggered riots and social unrest. Is there more trouble ahead?

For many people, particularly those living in wealthy countries, getting enough food to eat is not an everyday problem.

THE MAIN COURSE

Is the Earth's climate changing? In recent years, this has been one of the fiercest debates of all. Most scientists agree that a build-up of gases is stopping energy from the Sun escaping Earth's atmosphere. So the planet is rapidly warming. These "greenhouse" gases, including carbon dioxide (CO_2) and methane (CH_4), are pumped out by our cars and factories. Climate change threatens farmland and food supply at a time of population growth. At the same time, farming itself contributes to global warming (see page 15). So how can we manage all these crises and still get the food to the plate?

DROUGHT
Severe climate conditions, such as drought, can destroy crops and lead to food shortages.

"In the next 30 years, food supply and food security will be severely threatened if little or no action is taken to address climate change and the food system's vulnerability to climate change."

United Nations Academic Impact (UNAI) 2016

TOO MUCH OR TOO LITTLE?

Very many of the debates about food come back to the same basic problem. Some people in the world don't have enough food to eat, while others have too much. Food poverty exists in every nation, but is at its most severe in the world's least developed regions. These are the same regions that are expected to be under the greatest pressure from population increase and climate change.

An abundance of food is on display in the window of this Italian deli in New York. Some of this food will go to waste if it is not bought in time.

HUNGER OR WASTE?

Surely the main goal of global food production is to make sure that everyone has access to a basic amount of healthy food? If so, we can say that although things have improved over the last 25 years, the system is still not working. Hunger kills more people each year than the deadly illnesses of tuberculosis, malaria, and AIDS added together. This happens at a time when about one-third of all the food grown each year is simply wasted, lost, or thrown away.

OVERPRODUCTION
Too many of these apples have been grown, and they have been thrown away to rot in a garbage dump.

FOOD RATIONS

People line up at a food station in Krisrooa, Kenya, where they are given rations of food aid in response to a famine that affected much of East Africa in 2016–2017.

FOOD WASTE

A pile of vegetables lies rotting in a garbage can behind a supermarket. Every day, shops and supermarkets throw away tons of food because it has passed its sell-by date.

THE BIG ISSUES

There is a bigger picture to bear in mind when we discuss food matters. It is not just a question of who is rich and who is poor. We must examine farming methods, international economics, fair trade, and the ways in which food is sold and distributed to see if things could be done differently.

SUBSISTENCE OR CASH?

Farms come in all shapes and sizes. Some are little more than temporary plots of land, cleared from the forest by cutting or burning. About half a billion farms worldwide are small-scale farms. But there are also huge grain-producing farms run on an industrial scale, often on former prairie grasslands. There are single-crop plantations, growing anything from oil palms to coffee, bananas or pineapples.

SMALL FARM
Workers tend to crops on a small-scale farm in the South Nyanza district of Kenya.

GROWING YOUR OWN

Subsistence farming is small-scale, aiming to provide just enough food for the family or community. Any small amounts left over in a good year might be sold at the local market or exchanged for goods. Farming in this way provides much of the food consumed in remote rural areas of Africa, Asia, and Latin America.

NUMBER CRUNCH
In Kenya, in East Africa...
- About 70 percent of Kenyans work full- or part-time in farming.
- 75 percent of farming output comes from small farms or herding.
- 30 percent of Kenya's produced wealth (GDP) comes from farming.
- Cash crops for export include tea, coffee, and vegetables.

Farmers pick tea leaves in China's Jiangxi province. The leaves from this plantation will be processed, packaged, and sent to customers who live thousands of miles away.

SALE AND EXPORT

Cash crops are grown commercially, generally on larger-scale farms. They are sold on the wider market or exported. Farming on this scale is more efficient. It brings in money and investment, employs more people, and produces crops with a higher yield. On the down side, it may use up a lot of scarce water for irrigation. And relying on a single export crop can be risky. As global prices rise and fall, local communities may suddenly find themselves short of work. Extra costs on top of large-scale production include labor and transportation. Does it make sense for farmers in Kenya to be growing cut flowers for the European market rather than food crops for their own people? And if global warming is the big problem, why increase carbon emissions by flying asparagus all the way from Peru to London?

LET'S DISCUSS...
SUBSISTENCE FARMING

- is local and needs little transport.
- often uses sustainable farming methods.
- does not use as much water as large-scale farming to irrigate crops.

- lacks money for new projects, such as well-building.
- only produces small amounts of food.
- is vulnerable to droughts.

11

1 THE SCIENCE OF FARMING

People live a lot longer than they used to. This is largely because of improvements in farming and better healthcare. Scientific farming has been of huge benefit to humans. Is this the way to grow more food for the world's rising population levels?

AGRICULTURAL REVOLUTION

Scientific farming began in some parts of the world in the 1700s and 1800s, and great advances continue to this day. Farmers have learned more and more about crops and soil, and how to improve crops and animals by selective breeding.

New technology, tractors, and even computers have replaced human muscle and horse power. There are chemical pesticides and fertilizers. All these form the basis of modern commercial farming, or agribusiness.

Spraying chemicals can protect crops from pests and diseases, increasing yields. However, some pesticides may poison harmless wildlife, including the bees that play a vital role in pollinating many crops.

MEAT MEDICINE
At many farms around the world, livestock are fed with antibiotics and even growth hormones to increase the amount of milk and meat they produce.

NUMBER CRUNCH
The US has the largest chicken meat industry in the world. In 2015, the US produced more than 40 billion pounds of chicken meat.

FACTORY FARMING

Environmentalists complain that modern farming methods have often made fields more like factories. Over-intensive farming can damage and erode the soil. Too much irrigation can encrust the soil with salts, making it unproductive. Chemicals can drain off the fields and pollute rivers, or kill off bees and other insects that are needed to pollinate many food crops. Antibiotic medication for cattle may stay in the meat and enter the food chain. Poultry such as chickens and turkeys may be raised in huge numbers in cramped conditions and carry disease.

SUSTAINABLE FUTURE

The fault is not with the science itself, but with the way it is used. Scientists have also helped us analyze the big problems and have looked for solutions that are friendly to the environment. Farming that is self-sufficient, sustainable, and fits in with nature is called permaculture.

LET'S DISCUSS...
MODERN FARMING METHODS

• are designed to avoid waste.

• use the very latest technology.

• produce high crop yields.

• may pollute the natural environment.

• are often over intensive.

• may mistreat animals.

13

THE BEST USE OF LAND?

The debate about feeding hungry people goes further than how much food we should produce on our farms. We need to ask some basic questions about how we use the land and what we produce.

BEEF VERSUS SOYA?

Vegetarians and vegans have an ethical argument against the eating of meat. But there is another argument based on efficient land use. To raise cattle, farmers have to plant, harvest, and process crops to make food for the animals, and then use pasture land for grazing. Crops such as soya only need planting and harvesting. Raising beef can use up eight times as much water as growing soya.

Studies show that two acres (0.8 ha) of soya provide 22 times as much protein as two acres of beef cattle pasture.

SOYA

Soya beans are used to produce animal feed. Their oil is used in food manufacturing and for industrial applications, and they can even be used to make a milk substitute.

NUMBER CRUNCH

26 percent of the Earth's ice-free land surface is used for grazing livestock. 11 percent is used for growing crops. One-third of this crop-growing area is used for producing animal feed.

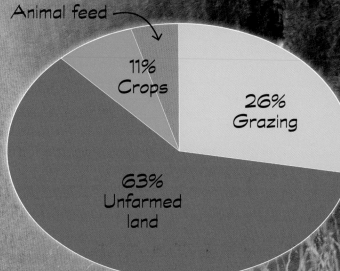

Animal feed

11% Crops

26% Grazing

63% Unfarmed land

A BURGER-FREE WORLD?

Did you know that about 2.4 million Big Macs are eaten worldwide every day? The market for meat is growing fast, especially in countries such as China, where the traditional diet was low on meat. Will a switch back ever be possible? Will we be forced to switch back in the interests of efficient land use?

GLOBAL BURGER

So many Big Macs are sold around the world that some economic organizations use it to compare the standard of living in different countries by showing how its cost varies from one country to another.

WATCH THE CARBON

Environmental protection is also an important part of better land use. Large areas of tropical forest are being cut down and given over to cattle ranching or oil palm plantations. This destruction of natural habitat makes global warming worse. It removes the forests that would soak up carbon dioxide. Composted soils full of organic matter may also absorb CO_2 better than degraded soils.

LET'S DISCUSS...
CATTLE RANCHING

- serves a growing demand for meat.
- naturally fertilizes pastures.
- can take place on land unsuitable for crops.

- uses up more fields and water than crops.
- produces less protein per two acres than soya.
- takes more time and money.

15

1 SCIENTIFIC SOLUTION?

DNA (deoxyribonucleic acid) is a molecule that carries nature's programming of life from one generation to the next. It is found in units called genes. Traditionally, farmers select the plants or animals with the most useful qualities to breed in order to improve the stock. Since the 1980s, scientists have been modifying the DNA of crops in order to add genetic characteristics that do not occur naturally.

COULD GM CROPS be the answer to increased demand and climate change, as suggested by some GM companies?

SUPPORTERS OF GENETIC MODIFICATION say that it is safe and isn't that different from the traditional practice of selective breeding. It can make a crop hardier, or more resistant to drought. It can make the crop more nutritious. It can make it resistant to pests or plant diseases. It can make the plant last longer, with a better shelf life.

GM CROPS have been widely adopted in the US and in many developing countries.

QUESTION IT!
ARE GM CROPS THE ANSWER TO OUR FOOD AND FARMING PROBLEMS?

GM CROPS can resist heavy doses of weedkiller that would kill a normal plant. This means that fewer chemicals need to be sprayed, and the soil does not need to be disturbed by lots of weeding.

IS IT TOO SOON TO CALL GM CROPS SAFE? GM crops remain banned in 38 countries and are grown in only 28.

IT IS HARD TO CONFINE GM CROPS within a particular area and to prevent them from cross-pollinating with wild plants or non-GM crops. This might affect the genetic make up of wild species, damaging biodiversity.

Pest-resistant plants might pose a threat to natural food chains.

A scientist in the US monitors the growth of a genetically modified crop bred in a laboratory.

GENETICALLY MODIFIED CROPS are unnecessary and are there to make money for a few giant corporations. New modifications are patented, which allows too much corporate power over global farming and food supply.

GM CROPS MAY THREATEN THE SURVIVAL of traditional crop strains that could be useful in the future.

THERE ARE FEARS THAT GM foods could create allergies and in the long term affect human health.

NUMBER CRUNCH
• 10 percent of the world's arable land is now sown with GM crops. In the US, 94 percent of maize and 94 percent of soya beans are GM.

2 PRODUCING THE FOOD

Farming is often the key to the whole economy of the countryside, or even of a whole nation, but it can be a risky business. A good harvest will depend on the weather, and the market prices for produce may go up and down. This uncertainty may become more extreme with future climate change, as traditional patterns of seasons become disrupted. Uncertainty threatens the security of the food supply.

French farmers protest against the plans by the French government to change the rules about financial subsidies to the farming industry.

HARD WORK
In many farms around the world, such as this one in Haiti, growing conditions are harsh and crop yields are low, making it hard for farmers to make a good living.

SUBSIDIZED FARMING

Despite the importance of food production, farmers themselves may make little profit. The costs of farming are high. Many countries or regions make special payments called subsidies to farmers. These aim to support farmers, bring stability and manage farming policy. Many farmers depend on subsidies, but critics claim these policies encourage waste or over-production. Subsidies can make the international market unfair. For example, the poor farmers of Haiti cannot compete with the price of US rice that has been grown with subsidies, and so Haiti has to import rice rather than grow its own.

FAIR TRADE

A movement for fairer international trade with less developed countries grew up in Europe in the 1960s. Today it campaigns politically for trade justice and also takes part in the market. It imports goods such as tea or coffee at an improved price to the farmer, with fair wages for the workers. It labels goods that meet these standards.

FAIR TRADE
A coffee farmer on the island of St. Helena picks ripe berries that will be made into coffee beans. Many coffee importers abide by trade agreements where growers are paid a fair price.

CHEAP LABOR

In many parts of the world, farmers keep down costs by paying low wages. Migrant workers are often employed with little job security. There are one to three million of them in the US alone. Worldwide, 60 percent of child laborers (aged 5-17) work in agriculture. Of these, 68 percent are family members working without pay.

LET'S DISCUSS...
SUBSIDIES FOR FARMERS

- stabilize the market by fixing prices.
- keep farmers in business by keeping them well-funded.
- help to plan and direct food production.

- may distort the reality of the market.
- may subsidize very rich farmers, not just those who need it.
- may give more developed countries an unfair advantage.

2 JUST ANOTHER COMMODITY?

Food is a basic need and a part of our everyday lives. It is also a commodity, something traded around the world to make money, in much the same way as oil or timber. Staple foods have long been treated as a commodity. About 2,000 years ago, ancient Rome depended on massive imports of grain from across its empire for its survival.

THE BUSINESS OF FOOD

Food as a commodity is part of a global finance system, which includes powerful banks. Critics of this system say that the price of food is manipulated for private profit, rather than in the interest of the producer or the consumer. There may be shortages and price hikes, or unsold produce piled up high in warehouses. Speculators bet on the future price of grain. They don't actually buy the commodity, they just gamble, like in a casino, on its value. This is called trading in futures.

Speculating in the "futures" market (below) may benefit banks and financial institutions, but it can drive up the prices of food around the world.

FROM FARM TO STORE

The farmer may grow the food, but is separated from the consumer by a long chain of processing and commercial deals. Each link in this chain adds to the final cost at the checkout. The food producer — and sometimes a whole nation of food producers — may be controlled by business interests. About 100 years ago, a US company called United Fruit became so powerful that it controlled much of Central America. The lands it "ruled" were nicknamed banana republics.

FAILING CROPS

This corn crop in Kenya has withered and died before it could be harvested. Failing crops can drive up the price of food.

NUMBER CRUNCH

In the year 2010, food demand rose by only 1.6 percent, but even so, food prices soared by a huge 25 percent.

SUPPLY AND DEMAND

Is this really the best way to organize our food supply? Banks and companies say it is. They point out that this system provides much needed finance and investment in farming and the food industry. They claim that unrestricted private trading or free trade in food commodities helps to keep prices down. When prices do rise, they say, it is not the fault of speculators but of rising demand and poor harvests.

LET'S DISCUSS... BIG BUSINESS

- invests in the whole food industry.
- uses competition to keep down prices.
- can act in the interests of farmers and consumers.

- wields huge amounts of power.
- puts profits before people.
- uncertainty can lead to an unstable market.

THE HARD SELL

A subsistence farmer plants seeds, grows the food, and eats it. The cost of the meal is labor and time. When someone in a developed country sits down at the table, the cost of the meal includes all sorts of items in addition to farming, such as transportation, processing, warehouse storage, packaging, distributing, advertising and marketing.

THE TRILLION DOLLAR INDUSTRY

The global grocery industry is massive, and growing fast. Some say it is too powerful. By 2020, it is expected to be worth $11.8 trillion. About ten global mega-corporations, such as Unilever, Nestlé, Pepsico, or Kellogg's, produce most of the branded foods we buy. They negotiate prices with giant supermarket chains such as Wal-mart. They compete with each other in turn to offer the cheapest price to customers, along with all sorts of special deals or cheaper own-brand offers.

FOOD GIANT

Swiss company Nestlé's products include baby food, bottled water, coffee, breakfast cereals, ice cream, pet food, and frozen food.

IS BIGGER BETTER?

Supermarkets are popular because they have everything under one roof, with easy parking and cheap prices. Online shopping for food, which is growing rapidly, is even more convenient. But supermarkets have their critics too. They are accused of wasting unsold food, of offering impersonal service, of storing too much data on people's personal shopping habits, and of taking business from family-owned stores, which cannot compete with these giant supermarkets.

COME AND BUY...

Many people prefer the hustle and bustle of their local famer's market or the ever-so-handy corner store to the large impersonal supermarkets. Small stores may specialize in ethnic or organic foods, or local produce. Farm shops or pick-your-own fruit outlets shortcut the whole lengthy process and get back to basics.

PILE HIGH, SELL CHEAP
Supermarket shelves are filled with produce. They need to sell in high volume to keep their prices down.

LET'S DISCUSS... SUPERMARKETS

Many of the foods on our supermarket shelves have to be produced in such large numbers that they can only be made in factories.

- can be easy to get to, particularly by car.
- have a huge range of foods in one place.
- can offer cheaper prices than small stores.

- take business away from local stores.
- waste food and packaging.
- offer low prices to suppliers.

23

2 LOSS LEADERS

In some parts of the world, it is common to see cattle wandering along a city street. Until recently, cattle could often be seen at open-air markets in the center of country towns in Britain or France. But it came as quite a shock to see two real live cows walking down the aisles of a supermarket in Stafford, England, in August 2015. This was part of a protest by farmers about the price of milk.

CAN WE EXPECT ANY PRODUCT to keep its value if demand declines? The market has to adjust by regulating the supply, changing the price, or cutting jobs.

PROFIT MARGINS OF SUPERMARKET FOODS are very tight indeed. For one supermarket chain to compete with its rivals, it has to sell its milk at the lowest possible price, which makes milk a well-known as a loss leader. That has to be good news for the consumer.

WHAT ELSE GOES INTO the cost of producing a gallon of milk? The retail price includes processing, packaging, transporting, and marketing. The farmer is not the only part of the equation.

QUESTION IT!
DO WE PAY ENOUGH FOR OUR MILK AT THE CHECKOUT?

SINCE 1995, milk delivered door-to-door in Britain had dropped from 45 percent to three percent of the market. The supermarkets had cornered the business. Were they now too powerful?

NUMBER CRUNCH
From 2004 to 2014, the US was the third largest dairy exporter in the world. But in 2015, dairy exports dropped by 30 percent due to changes in the global market. A country's food industry can change quickly!

French farmers protest in the city of Lyon, demanding that stores and supermarkets pay a fair price for their milk.

DURING THE 2015 PROTEST IN BRITAIN, the farmers complained that the supermarkets were dictating the terms to the companies and cooperatives that sold their milk. They feared for their future — and the future of farming in Britain. Who won the argument? The supermarkets raised the minimum price offered to the farmers.

HUNGRY WORLD

The United Nations estimates that one out of every nine people in the world is undernourished. That's about 795 million people. Most of them live in developing countries, especially in Africa south of the Sahara and in Southern Asia. But there are also millions of undernourished people living in developed countries.

GOOD NEWS, BAD NEWS

The statistic is shocking, but the good news is that it is about half of the number of 25 years ago. The goal now is to make food poverty a thing of the past. But that's a tall order. Food shortages are often the result of poverty and inequality. Sometimes they happen when a government tries — but fails — to reform land ownership, farming, or distribution of food. Wars and natural disasters are all too common. Drought or floods, which are affected by climate change, may destroy crops.

REFUGEES
People wait for aid in the Dadaab refugee camp in Kenya. These refugees have fled neighboring Somalia in search of food.

MORE PEOPLE NEED MORE FOOD

The world population currently stands at 7.4 billion. The UN expects it to reach 9.7 billion by 2050, rising to perhaps 11.2 billion by 2100. It predicts that a great increase in food production will be necessary to meet the needs of all those people.

NEW OPTIONS

One way forward would be to cut out so much waste. The developed countries of the world currently waste the same amount each year as all the food grown in Africa south of the Sahara. Interesting new technologies are being developed too. In the desert in South Australia, tomatoes are already being grown in special greenhouses. Sun reflected from mirrors is used to desalinate sea water. The salt is removed by distillation so that pure water can be used to water the crop.

UNDER GLASS

These tomatoes are ripening in a greenhouse in Ukraine. Greenhouses allow plants to grow in controlled conditions and protect them from temperature extremes.

With the planet warming, weather conditions may become more volatile, with terrible floods in some regions and extended droughts in others, as this farmer in Thailand is experiencing.

LET'S DISCUSS...
GLOBAL HUNGER

- has already been greatly reduced.
- is being targeted by the UN.
- needs new approaches and methods from farmers and farming.

- still affects millions of people.
- may be made worse by population growth.
- may be made worse by the effects of climate change.

THE FEAR OF FAMINE

When a famine strikes, news reports show heartbreaking pictures of babies suffering, exhausted parents seeking medical aid, and people battling through dust storms with their wells dry, their crops ruined, and their cattle dead. Every continent has suffered from famine at some point in history, but it is often in the dry, hot lands that the crisis strikes hardest.

NUMBER CRUNCH

The 1983-85 famine in Ethiopia killed about 400,000 people. Famine-related issues cost Ethiopia about $ 1.1 billion every year between 1997 and 2007.

EMERGENCY ACTION

Famine relief may be carried out by United Nations agencies, the International Red Cross and Red Crescent Movement, and by many charity organisations such as Oxfam. Many people around the world raise funds when a crisis strikes, to send in emergency medical teams and aid workers. The obvious need might seem to be for supplies of food, but these can take too long to reach the right place. If the cost of food is the problem rather than supply, it might make sense to give people cash or food vouchers. Starving children need special milk powder or a nutritional paste to recover, before they can take solid food.

STOPPING FAMINE BEFORE IT HAPPENS

Prevention is the best cure, and it costs less too. It's called disaster risk reduction, which may mean better management of water resources, improving food distribution, economic planning, or conflict resolution. Ethiopia has had a long history of catastrophic famines. Working with the World Bank, the Ethiopian government has brought in a system of giving hungry people the chance to work for food or money. If disaster strikes in one region, then a neighboring region can sell locally sourced food to the international relief agencies.

IRISH FAMINE
This monument commemorates the Great Famine in Ireland between 1845 and 1852, which killed approximately 1 million people.

While young people are able to move away from famine-hit regions, the elderly and ill are unable to travel and must stay behind, relying on aid or anything distant relatives can send to them.

LET'S DISCUSS... FAMINE

- charities raise funds for doctors and volunteers.
- is devastating, but quick action saves lives.
- is preventable with good planning.

- has killed millions of people over the ages.
- is closely related to poverty.
- is a real danger as the global population increases.

29

3 HELP FROM ABROAD

Foreign aid is the help given by countries or international organizations to the governments of other countries. It can take various forms, but many of these relate to food production and supply. The aid may include food, money, loans, training, or medical assistance.

FOOD SUPPLIES MAY SAVE LIVES in an emergency, such as famine or a natural disaster.

INTERNATIONAL ASSISTANCE is generally a good thing in itself, making the world a more secure and friendly place. It saves lives and helps the poor.

FARMING EQUIPMENT OR TRAINING will help food production and trade in the long term.

NUMBER CRUNCH

In 2015, the US gave $2.5 billion worth of emergency and development food aid to the world's least developed countries.

RELIEF OF POVERTY will help prevent food shortage and famine, and also reduce the growth in population.

> "Food aid can help to lift developing nations out of poverty, promote political stability and economic growth. It must be structured efficiently to achieve its objective."
>
> Editorial, *Chicago Tribune* 2013

QUESTION IT!
IS OVERSEAS AID A GOOD IDEA?

OVERSEAS AID TIED TO military alliances may only create more conflict, increasing the likelihood of food poverty or famine.

DOES AID ENCOURAGE DEPENDENCY rather than self-sufficiency?

CRITICS SAY that in many countries the aid is pocketed by corrupt rulers and government officials, and never reaches the ordinary people it is meant for.

WILL AID FOR INDUSTRIAL DEVELOPMENT increase the emission of greenhouse gases and add to global warming?

AID IN THE FORM OF LOANS serves the interests of the giver more than the receiver, who will become deeper in debt and even poorer.

THE RIGHT STUFF

The effects of extreme hunger in some of the world's poorest communities are shocking. We might assume that all is well in the more developed countries. Well, there are people short of food there, too. But even amongst those with plenty to eat, there are problems with what they consume. Many people have a diet that is unhealthy or unbalanced.

BODY FUEL

The body needs the right mix of fuel, just like a car. It needs all sorts of nutrients. Carbohydrates include starch, found in bread, rice, pasta, or potatoes. Starch and sugars break down to form glucose, which in the blood mixes with the oxygen we breathe to give us energy. Fats, found in meat, oil, and dairy products, are carbohydrates too. Proteins, found in fish, eggs, cheese, and meat, build and repair body cells. What else? High-fiber foods to help digestion, minerals such as iron and calcium, and vitamins, the chemicals that help release energy from nutrients.

NUMBER CRUNCH

This plate diagram was created by the United States Department of Agriculture to show the proportion of vegetables, fruits, grains, meat, and dairy that should make up a healthy diet.

KEEP IT FRESH
Food markets, such as this one in London, offer a wide range of fresh produce.

STRIKING A BALANCE

Are you a picky eater? A balanced diet of fresh food, offering a good variety of nutrients, should keep you healthy and in good shape, without any need for supplements such as vitamin pills or protein shakes. Plenty of exercise and moderate portions are good ideas, too!

Many people do need special diets. For instance, if they have specific medical needs or allergies. Others may choose a vegetarian or vegan diet, or follow religious rules about what they may eat. It is still possible for all these people to keep to a balanced diet.

Some schools like this one in Malaysia teach the importance of fresh food by encouraging children to grow vegetables either in special gardens or at home.

LET'S DISCUSS... A BALANCED DIET

- includes a wide range of nutrients.
- includes lots of fiber to keep your guts healthy.
- is rich in minerals and vitamins.

- prevents malnutrition.
- helps prevent health problems such as heart disease and bowel disease.

PROCESSING AND ADDITIVES

We all like to keep fresh food and ingredients in the fridge. Or do we? Many people have to admit that they're more likely to eat more processed or ready prepared foods, especially if these look tasty and don't involve too much work. Of course it is fine to have a pizza or a pie from time to time, but a diet based on junk food or candy really is a bad idea.

FATS, SUGAR, SALT

People's craving for fatty and sweet foods probably dates back to the time when these were in short supply, and humans needed fats and sugars for energy. Sugar can be good for you, but far too much of it is added to our food and drinks, sometimes in the form of super-sweet high-fructose corn syrup (HFCS). Our snacks and convenience foods are overloaded with salt. We need to eat fat, too, but some kinds, such as saturated fats and hydrogenated oils or trans fats, may be harmful — scientists are still debating what may or may not be safe.

NUMBER CRUNCH

A can of soda might contain up to 13 teaspoons of sugar.

Microwavable meals may be easy to cook and ready to eat in a few minutes, but some of them contain high levels of salt, fats, and sugars.

A COMBINATION OF CHEMICALS

If you look more closely at the labels of some of your favorite foods, you may be in for a shock. The list of ingredients looks like they belong in a science lab. Which they do. They include all sorts of chemical additives. There are preservatives, colorants, flavorings, and texturants. They have little or no value as nutrition. Some are downright harmful, and some have already been banned.

COLORFUL
Many treats and snacks contain a mix of artificial chemicals to make them brightly colored.

ATTRACTIVE PACKAGING
Many brands of snacks, candy, and drinks have bright and colorful packaging so that they stand out on the crowded supermarket shelves.

THE RISKS
Bad fats raise the levels of cholesterol, and the risk of heart disease. Salt raises your blood pressure. Sugar increases the risk of Type 2 diabetes, obesity and heart disease. You can monitor how much of each food type you eat by checking the labels on food packaging.

LET'S DISCUSS... SUGAR

- is needed to provide energy.
- should be eaten in very small amounts.
- helps make food such as ice cream taste nice.

- is found in bread, soups and sauces as well as in sweets.
- rots our teeth and can make us overweight.
- increases the risk of Type 2 diabetes and heart disease.

35

4 THE BODY-MASS INDEX

The body-mass index compares a person's height with their mass (or weight) to see how they rate on the scale. Obesity is in the news these days. The problem is common in the more developed countries.

WHY OBESITY?

Obesity may be caused by a medical condition or by genetic makeup, but it is often related to eating too much food, the wrong kind of food, or policies of the food industry or government — which can make some unhealthy foods cheap and healthy foods expensive. Obesity is a problem to be solved, and should not be met with hostility or a lack of understanding.

REGULAR OR LARGE?

The marketing of supersized food portions began with buckets of popcorn in US cinemas at the end of the 1960s. Today we all know about gigantic fountain drinks, about the ever growing size of chocolate bars, about giant portions of pizza or fried chicken. The more people eat, the more they get used to eating too much.

EATING DISORDERS

Anxiety about appearance is widespread. Advertising emphasises extremely thin fashion models. Magazines offer fad diets that don't always work. Stress about a wide range of issues may lead to psychological problems affecting control of the digestive system. These eating disorders include anorexia nervosa, bulimia, and binge eating disorder (BED).

SCHOOL MEALS

Some schools and education boards have been criticized for providing unhealthy school meals. People have campaigned to replace these with healthier options.

NUMBER CRUNCH

One-third of all young Americans (aged 6–19) are rated as overweight or obese.

Amateur athletes take part in the 2016 Hunger Run in Rome to raise money for food relief programs around the world. Many people exercise regularly to avoid becoming unfit and obese.

LET'S DISCUSS... PORTION SIZE

- eating moderately will make us feel better.
- supersized options have already been removed from some food outlets.

- large portions encourage overeating and waste. Restaurants could introduce a "small" portion option.

GOVERNMENT INTERFERENCE

Isn't it up to us how we eat? Surely that is a basic, individual right? Or should the government do more to control or influence our diet by passing laws or putting taxes on unhealthy foods? Critics of government intervention complain of a "nanny state," forever interfering in the lives of individuals and bossing them around. Supporters say that's what they're elected to do — to make society healthier.

WE DON'T COMPLAIN when laws are passed to make sure that food outlets are hygienic. So why complain if a government looks for ways to make us eat and drink more healthily? Unhealthy foods have a huge impact on the costs of medical care and treatment of diseases.

THE WORLD HEALTH ORGANIZATION is urging countries to tax sugary soft drinks. In 2017, the government of Portugal will do just that, raising the cost of a standard can of soda. This tax is expected to raise money for the public health service.

LABELLING OF FOODS with a simple health warning, making lists of ingredients easier to understand, or labelling food if it is genetically modified, empowers the consumer. The British Medical Association recommends a "traffic light" warning for fats, sugars, and salts, with red as "high," yellow as "medium," and green as "low."

AS THINGS STAND, it is not up to us what we get to eat anyway, but up to the rich and powerful food industry, which lobbies governments.

THE FOOD INDUSTRY EMPLOYS many people and is good for the economy. We should not be punishing it with too many taxes and regulations. If the industry wasn't selling what the public wanted, nobody would be buying its products.

IS IT RIGHT TO TAX SUGARY DRINKS when a certain amount of sugar is acceptable? If I am only buying one sugary drink a week, why should I pay extra tax on it? It is up to me to balance my diet.

HEALTH WARNINGS ON FOOD ITEMS, such as the "traffic light" system, are too simplistic, and might push people away from buying perfectly healthy options as part of a more balanced diet.

QUESTION IT!
IS IT RIGHT FOR GOVERNMENTS TO TELL US WHAT TO EAT?

SHOULDN'T IT BE UP to us as thinking individuals to decide what we eat for ourselves, rather than being told?

FOOD FOR ALL?

Debates are about arguing — not for the sake of it, but for a purpose. There are many good stories to be told about food, and while this book focuses on the problems, the end purpose of these debates is to be positive, looking at ways in which the world can bring about food security. This term is a modern one, but really the idea is a very old one — making sure that everyone has enough to eat.

AIMING FOR THE FUTURE

The UN's Food and Agriculture Organisation (FAO) organized World Summit meetings on food security in Rome in 1996, 2002, and 2009. It declared that food security *"exists when all people, at all times, have physical and economic access to sufficient, safe and nutritious food to meet their dietary needs and food preferences for an active and healthy life."*

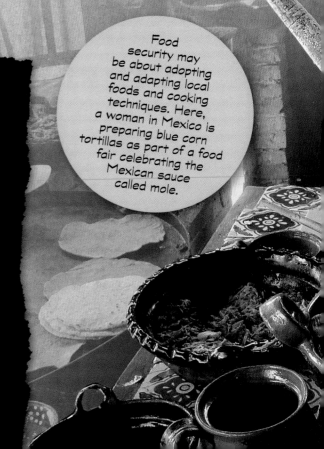

Food security may be about adopting and adapting local foods and cooking techniques. Here, a woman in Mexico is preparing blue corn tortillas as part of a food fair celebrating the Mexican sauce called mole.

ZERO HUNGER 2030?

It's a hopeful vision, especially given the global scale of the problem, the soaring population and the changing climate. Food security can only be brought about by a huge international effort. Luckily, there has never been greater cooperation between nations, working together through the UN's World Food Program. World leaders have set 2030 as the target date for "zero hunger." Can it be done?

PEACE, TOO

If you watch television news, a threat to food security comes up nearly every night. All over the world there are conflicts and wars. Cutting off food supply is often used as a bargaining counter in international political crises. War and bombing cuts off food to civilians. Fields lie unused, full of landmines or cluster bombs. Millions of people are forced to flee their homes. The UN and many other organizations do all they can to prevent conflict and help the hungry. Yes, zero hunger might be achieved, although 2030 is a tough deadline. But world leaders should remember that an essential ingredient for food security is… security.

SAFE AND SOUND?

The political upheaval in many parts of the world, such as Syria and regions of Africa, places huge strain on food supplies. People are forced from one place to another to find safety. These people from Syria have found refuge in a camp in Turkey.

LET'S DISCUSS…
THE WORLD'S NATIONS

- are working together through the UN.
- are aiming for zero hunger by 2030, and…
- could possibly make it happen.

- may halt food supplies during political disputes.
- may threaten food security during wars.
- must give peace a chance.

41

WORLD FOOD DAY

World Food Day is held each year on October 16. It marks the founding of the Food and Agriculture Organization of the UN in Canada, in 1945. Its focus is on raising awareness of global hunger and on activities that individuals and groups can do to campaign and raise funds. The slogan of World Food Day 2016 was *"Climate is changing. Food and agriculture must too."*

This NASA image shows how a base on Mars may be set up to grow food for astronauts living there.

FOOD, GLORIOUS FOOD

While we campaign for the right kind of change, we should remember to celebrate the wider story. Food is so much more than nutrition. It is rooted in our history, our traditions and cultures, our family life and friendships. Remember the pleasure of good cooking, or the bite of a fresh apple. And once in a while, we can even allow ourselves a bag of popcorn, too! When we try out dishes from other parts of the world, it is like an international conversation.

SPACE SALAD

Food is about how we use our planet and how we ourselves exist. It is central to many world faiths, which focus on fasting as well as feasting.

Food has always seized the imagination of artists, politicians, farmers ,and scientists. As soon as humans got into space, scientists started finding out how to grow plants in the spacecraft.

ONE OF THESE DAYS

When the day comes when there is enough food for a poor family in New York, for a goat herder in Mali, for a child on the streets of Kolkata, for a poor farmer in Vietnam, then World Food Day really will be something we can all celebrate.

LET'S DISCUSS... TRADITIONAL FOODS

- are part of our culture.
- have great international variety.
- are best homemade.

- are being rejected for processed foods.
- are sometimes thought to take "too long" to prepare.
- are being replaced by ready-prepared meals.

43

5 RIGHTS FOR FOOD

Human rights are the basic requirements for a happy, healthy, and fair life. They may be rights we wish for, rights we have and need to defend, or rights that are the basis of national or international laws. They are often criticized, but are essential as a checklist of justice and human progress.

ENOUGH GOOD, healthy, and appropriate food should be readily available.

THE SUPPLY OF FOOD should be secure and sustainable for present and future generations.

YES, IT SHOULD AND IT IS. Its importance is recognized in the Universal Declaration of Human Rights, the International Convention of the Rights of the Child, the International Covenant on Economic, Social and Cultural Rights, and the European Convention on Human Rights.

FOOD SHOULD BE ACCESSIBLE AND AFFORDABLE, in the right place at the right time.

QUESTION IT!
SHOULD FOOD BE CALLED A HUMAN RIGHT?

HUMAN RIGHTS ALL SOUND VERY WORTHWHILE, but the fact that people remain hungry around the world shows that they can be too easily ignored.

THE LAWS IN WHICH HUMAN RIGHTS are embedded are often too complicated or unenforceable in practice.

These people are serving food at a homeless shelter in the UK.

FOOD IS JUST A TRADED COMMODITY like any other. Is it really a human rights issue?

POWERFUL CORPORATIONS, dictatorial governments, or corrupt officials have little regard for the human rights of an individual.

"the fundamental right of everyone to be free from hunger... To improve methods of production, conservation and distribution of food by making full use of technical and scientific knowledge, by disseminating knowledge of the principles of nutrition and by developing or reforming agrarian systems in such a way as to achieve the most efficient development and utilization of natural resources... an equitable distribution of world food supplies in relation to need."

from the International Covenant on Economic, Social and Cultural Rights 11.2, adopted by the United Nations in 1966

45

GLOSSARY

ADDITIVE
A substance added to food to improve or preserve it. Additives are not a natural part of food.

AGRIBUSINESS
Farming business organized on an industrial scale for commercial profit.

ALLERGY
An abnormal reaction of the body to a substance that is harmless to most other people.

ANIMAL WELFARE
The caring, proper treatment of animals.

ANTIBIOTIC
A medicine that stops the spread of harmful micro-organisms. Farm animals may be treated with antibiotics to keep them free from disease.

BIODIVERSITY
The variety of plant and animal life in an area. A large variety is a sign of a thriving environment.

BODY MASS INDEX
A measure of whether someone is over- or underweight.

CALCIUM
A mineral that we need for healthy teeth and bones.

CARBOHYDRATE
The sugars and starches that form the main source of energy in the diet.

CASH CROPS
Crops that are grown commercially, rather than for local use by the farmer or the community.

CHOLESTEROL
A waxy, fat-like compound that is present in food and is also made in the liver. Too much cholesterol may lead to narrowing of the arteries that supply blood to the heart.

CLIMATE CHANGE
Any major change in the global climate. Most scientists believe that the burning of fossil fuels such as coal and gas is making the Earth warmer.

COLORANTS
A pigment or chemical added to food to give it an attractive color.

COMMODITY
Something that can be bought or sold.

DESALINATE
The removal of salt from water. Various industrial processes are used to remove salt from seawater.

DIET
The kinds of foods a person, a community, or an animal normally eats.

DISTILLATION
Purifying a liquid, such as water, by a process of heating and cooling.

EATING DISORDERS
Mental health problems that result in abnormal eating habits. For example, anorexia nervosa is an obsessive desire to avoid food and lose weight. Bulimia is the desire to eat excessively, followed by deliberate vomiting or fasting.

EROSION
The wearing away by wind, rain, or other causes. Over-intensive farming can cause soil to erode.

ETHICAL
Avoiding activities that harm people, animals, or the environment.

FAIR TRADE
Trade between developed countries and developing countries in which the local producers are paid a fair price.

FERTILIZER
A chemical or natural substance added to land to increase its fertility.

FOOD CHAIN
A series of organisms that are each dependent on the next as a source of food.

FOOD POVERTY
When someone cannot obtain a nutritious diet, either because they cannot afford healthy food or because they live in an area where healthy food is difficult to find.

FOOD SECURITY
Having secure access to enough affordable, nutritious food.

FREE TRADE
International trade without tariffs (taxes on goods) or other government restrictions.

GREENHOUSE GASES
Gases that cause the greenhouse effect, which is the trapping in Earth's atmosphere of more energy from the Sun. Major greenhouse gases include methane and carbon dioxide.

HIGH-FRUCTOSE CORN SYRUP
A cheap, very fattening sweetener made from corn starch that is often used in junk food.

HYDROGENATED OILS
Oils used in food that have been treated with hydrogen in order to reduce some of the harmful saturated fats.

IRRIGATION
Supplying water to land to help grow crops.

LOBBIES
Organized groups of people who try to influence governments or lawmakers.

MIGRANT WORKER
A person who moves to another country in order to look for work.

NUTRIENT
A substance found in food that is vital for life and growth.

OBESITY
Being overweight. Obesity can cause serious health problems, such as heart disease and diabetes.

OVER-INTENSIVE FARMING
The spoiling of land by the over-use of fertilizers and pesticides, or by poor land management, which may degrade soil and make it less fertile.

PASTURE
Grassland suitable for grazing farm animals, especially cattle and sheep.

PESTICIDE
A substance used to destroy insects or other organisms harmful to crops or farm animals.

POLLINATE
Depositing pollen on a flower or a plant to allow fertilization. Many crops are pollinated by insects.

PRESERVATIVES
Substances added to food to prevent decay.

PROFIT MARGIN
The amount by which a business's income exceeds its costs.

PROTEIN
A molecule, found in meat, fish, nuts, and eggs, that is essential for the body's growth and repair.

SATURATED FATS
A fat that is usually solid at room temperature, such as butter. Too much saturated fat is considered unhealthy in a diet.

STAPLE
A main or important part of someone's diet, for example rice or bread.

SUBSISTENCE FARMING
Growing crops or raising animals only to feed oneself, with nothing left over to trade.

TRADING IN FUTURES
Buying and selling commodities at an agreed price, with payment and delivery occurring at a future date (by which time the commodity's value may have risen or fallen).

VITAMINS
Any of the organic substances that are essential to the nutrition of most animals. For example, vitamin C, found in citrus fruits such as oranges, keeps the body's cells and tissues healthy.

INDEX

PICTURE CREDITS